101 WAYS

TO STAY OFF THE

IRS RADAR

Abby Eisenkraft, EA

Parker House Publishing

This material is for informational and entertainment purposes only. It is not intended to be a substitute for tax, accounting or financial advice from a professional. Presentation of this information is not intended to create nor constitute a professional tax relationship. Readers are advised not to act upon this information without doing the appropriate research and/or seeking the service of a credentialed tax professional.

Neither the publisher nor the author shall be liable for any physical, psychological, emotional, financial, or commercial damages, including but not limited to special, incidental, consequential or other damages. Our views and rights are the same: You are responsible for your own choices, actions and results.

ISBN 978-0-69-282457-3

ACKNOWLEDGEMENTS

Throughout my journey in tax, I have been fortunate to have had many mentors. These people all gave their time generously because of their true love of this profession. A huge thank you to the following: Frank Agostino, Norman Barotz, Warren Bernstein, Robert Genovese, Jack Gold, and Mark Klein.

Carolita Johnson is the illustrator who did several of the cartoons in this book including the cover. I really enjoy her work. She is truly a great talent!

The other cartoons were collaborations with Isha Shinde, whose talent and patience I am grateful for.

To my friends who have always been so supportive throughout this process and have kept me accountable (pardon the pun - sorry, couldn't resist), thank you all, especially Glenda V. and Audrey Kirwin.

And, of course, to my family, who always made me feel that I could do anything. Bet you didn't see this coming.

Contents

INTRODUCTION 1

UNREPORTED INCOME (Or So It Would Appear)..........11

FOREIGN ISSUES - The IRS Has a Long Arm! 31

SWEET CHARITY..41

FORMS YOU RECEIVED OR SHOULD HAVE FILED 47

NO, THAT'S NOT DEDUCTIBLE 65

MISTAKES ON YOUR TAX RETURN –

INTENTIONAL OR NOT...83

CONCLUSION 101

RESOURCES.. 105

ABOUT THE AUTHOR... 107

This is where we audit you for all eternity.

INTRODUCTION

Few things elicit fear more than the word "audit." It shakes you right to the core. Visions of IRS interrogations bring most people to tears.

The thought of digging through tons of paperwork for a past year you don't even remember, losing work time, or trying to find skilled representation is not something that anyone looks forward to.

For every dollar that the IRS spends on enforcement, they collect about seven dollars. While the IRS budget has been severely cut by Congress, enforcement is not going away any time soon – it's profitable! It brings in revenue!

In-person audits, which are more of a drain on IRS resources, usually happen because the IRS believes that they potentially will get more money if they haul in the taxpayer for a face-to-face interview.

Speaking of bringing additional revenue, just look at some of the amnesty programs the IRS has rolled out over the years in the area of unreported foreign accounts. With one of the first rounds in the post-UBS-scandal world, the first voluntary disclosure program brought in billions of dollars to the IRS. The IRS was shocked at how many people came forward. Since that initial program, they have rolled out a number of other similar programs, with scared people coming forward in droves hoping to avoid criminal charges, massive penalties, etc.

As of this printing, the Internal Revenue Service has recently announced that to date, via their Offshore Voluntary Compliance effort, more than 100,000 taxpayers have come into compliance, reporting their previously unreported overseas accounts, paying over $10 billion in taxes, interest and penalties since 2009.

As an Enrolled Agent, a federally licensed tax practitioner enrolled to practice before the IRS, I have been representing clients before the Taxing Authorities for more a decade. Over the years, there have been changes in the types of audit, the manner in which audits are conducted, their targets, and means of resolution. But one thing is certain – the clients who are chosen for audit are rarely randomly chosen. We'll talk more about that later.

However, an audit is not the end of the world. The IRS has the right to request substantiation for ANY item reported on a tax return. And you just have to think of it that way, as hard as it is not to take it personally. Even though you are chosen to be audited, it does not necessarily mean you did anything wrong on your tax return, or that you will owe money; I have represented numerous clients in audits where I was able to get them thousands of dollars back from the IRS. Why? Because the taxpayer made mistakes on the tax return they prepared.

For most people, an audit is not life-altering; they learn a lot, they will certainly keep their records better in the future, and they survive.

I have worked with taxpayers who come into my office howling, "Why am I being audited?" And in looking over their tax returns, I ask them – "Why would you NOT be audited?"

I have seen it all. Crazy deductions people make up with their friends; "kitchen table" tax preparers with no training, license or designation who create fake deductions to inflate a refund for a client (and they are not even signing the tax returns either, which is required by law if they are paid!); preparers who PROMISE refunds of a specific dollar amount ("How would you like an $8,000 refund?"), etc. Often, all I need to do is look at the first two pages of these tax returns, and I already know why the client is being audited, and often, what the outcome of that audit will be.

How many times have I heard:

But I wear black to work! That's a uniform!
Well, my friend told me...
I go to the gym. Deduct that!
Deduct my cable TV – I watch TV for work sometimes.
My internet – I use it sometimes for work.
My personal cell phone – I make business calls.
My wife is my dependent.
I am single but head of household – I pay the bills!
I had to dry clean my work suits.
My hair, my nails – I have to look a certain way for work.

Sigh...these are all wrong assumptions and you've come to the right place to find out why.

But back to audits.

There is more than one type of audit. It doesn't start with a knock on your door either, unless the IRS (or State) has repeatedly tried to reach you, and you have ignored them. There are correspondence audits (which transpire by mail), there are desk audits (at the IRS), and there are field audits (perhaps at your place of business or the office of your preparer). And if you are thinking, "Do they do home visits?" the answer is yes. True case - I had a client who hired me after trying to handle her own audit. She screamed at the IRS, telling them she had nothing to hide and if they didn't believe her, to come over. And you know what? They did!

Some of the smallest of things can lead to a correspondence audit, and we'll talk about that in this book.

In this era of massive identity theft, it's important to know if it's really the IRS requesting information. Every day there is a new scam, from threatening phone calls to fake notices to fake emails demanding money to fraudsters boldly coming to the doors of unassuming taxpayers and threatening them in person. And it will only get worse. The IRS recently announced that they will again start using outside collection agencies to assist them. How will the public be able to discern who is real and who is a fraudster? The IRS has stated that they will send a letter first, but many people in tax trouble don't open their mail from the IRS.

As this book goes to print, there are fraudsters dressed as troopers, with a car that resembles a squad car, coming right up to the homes of innocent victims whom they scare into making immediate payments. These people are not the Taxing Authorities. Tell them you need to close the door because the attack dogs are a bit agitated, and then call the police. If it truly is a representative from the federal or state taxing authority, they will leave a business card, and you can check on the authenticity.

The classic scam is a phone call threatening to cart you off to jail unless you provide a credit card this very instant, amid screeching sirens and other inducements for on-the-spot payment. You cannot imagine how many clients I had to talk off the ledge because they were absolutely convinced their time had come. It took a lot of convincing on my part before they stopped hyperventilating and actually believed me. These scam calls are terrifying because they convince really smart people to do really foolish things.

This is a very serious problem, and it is important for people to be aware not only of the scams but of how to deal with the real IRS. There are ways to stay off the IRS radar. The starting point is knowledge and I am happy to help get you started.

My hope is that you will not only be entertained by this book, but you will learn something. And knowledge is power. You may save yourself thousands of dollars, too. Should you ever be on the receiving end of an audit notice, the first thing to do is to breathe. Calmly try to figure out what is being questioned, if the notice is legitimate, and the best way to substantiate what you deducted. And if you need tax help, make sure it's someone qualified in this area. Not just someone who is going to carry in your receipts, but someone who will analyze, strategize, and fight for your rights. I remember one audit where I saved the client $100,000 after a very long and drawn-out fight with an auditor. This auditor told me he absolutely did not believe the client, and was going to penalize her and was not going to budge, even if I go to a Supervisor. I fought him relentlessly on this particular point for weeks, until he finally agreed to remove the penalty from the audit report. When we were done, he said to me that he hoped that my client appreciated me because I worked so hard for her. (A shocking statement from the IRS!) But let's give credit where it's due. It took two. Here was a reasonable auditor who was dead set against granting the client relief for a number of valid reasons, but I asked that he just consider the very special extenuating circumstances of the case, and he did. We both did well by the client. There are a lot of good, hard-working folks at the IRS who are willing to work with taxpayers and their representatives to resolve the tax issues. And a

lot of crazy people, too, as well as dangerously misinformed people who give out wrong information to the public.

The Taxing Authorities have their job to do and I have mine.

Now that you have some background as to the types of audits that you might encounter, let's review some triggers and traps, so you can stay off the IRS radar.

"But I don't work!"

UNREPORTED INCOME
(Or So It Would Appear)

1. YOU HAVE A CASH BUSINESS

Newsflash – taxpayers are required to report all worldwide income from any and every source. Even if you don't deposit the cash, you are not off the hook for reporting it. The IRS has the tools and capability to detect and estimate your income.

Do you think that even if you get caught, they will only look for a few years? In the case of fraud, there is no statute of limitations, and they can go back as far as they deem necessary.

It doesn't matter how you receive the income – bank wire, cash, check, credit card, barter, PayPal, Bitcoin – income is always reportable unless there is something in the IRS code specifically stating that it is not.

2. NO SUCH THING AS "OFF THE BOOKS"

If you received compensation for a service you performed, but didn't receive a Form W-2, Form

1099-Miscellaneous, Form 1099-K, etc., you still must report the income. An employer may send it at a later date, or not at all, but if that employer ever gets audited and files it late with the IRS, suddenly there's a record. And if you didn't report it, you have a problem on your hands. What will you tell an IRS Examiner? "I thought it was off the books!"

There are numerous ways for the Taxing Authorities to pick up on unreported income. They can look at your lifestyle, your bank accounts, other financial accounts, etc. They can talk to other people, receive information from whistleblowers, etc.

If you are expecting a reporting form but don't receive it, and you are unable to obtain it from an employer, you may be able to obtain it via an IRS transcript. You can make a request, and there are certain procedures to follow when the W-2 is missing.

3. LOW INCOME

Does your low income make sense?

It might. Let's say you are an actor or a musician, and not yet a great success. Your income is low, and after expenses, one wonders how you had money to eat. Be prepared to show a paper trail of exhausted savings, family support, etc. If you got paid in cash for a gig, it is reportable.

I did an audit for a young couple. The husband was a musician and the wife was a journalist, both self-employed. The IRS was absolutely convinced that there HAD to be unreported income for this young couple to afford to live in New York City, and even quantified what they believed to be unreported income in the initial audit. This couple lived quite modestly and were recently married. Their original records were not in good order, and I gave them a crash course in required IRS recordkeeping, and how to properly organize supporting documentation. We proved to the IRS that the couple received family support, and cash wedding gifts. We were able to eliminate the proposed unreported income and greatly reduce the amount owed to the IRS for items they couldn't support. They are now my very organized clients.

But keep in mind that the Taxing Authorities can do a lifestyle audit and base certain assumptions on where and how you live.

4. EARNED INCOME CREDIT (EIC) FRAUD

How does one commit EIC fraud? You come up with a fake business or don't report all of your business

income, reporting just enough income to qualify for the Earned Income Credit, which can result in a refund of a few thousand dollars.

After years of giving out credits that were fraudulently obtained, the IRS has become very tough in this area, and have implemented more stringent requirements for proof. This has become a sore spot for them, and you may be subject to civil fraud penalties for this violation, and worse. It's quite easy to spot these fraudulent tax returns, because conveniently, they all hit the "sweet spot" in terms of the right income and not a penny more.

There are a lot of fraudulent preparers that specialize in EIC fraud. And guess what? They go to jail, too.

If you have a business, make sure that you have the proper documentation to prove the income and expenses that qualify you for the Earned Income Credit.

If you have children that qualify you for the Earned Income credit, they need to be yours, not the neighbors' children, or a relative trying to help you out, etc. You need to be able to prove they truly live with you, and if they are children of other family members, be prepared to explain why you are claiming them, and show detailed records proving that they live with you, your address is on file with their school, etc. The requisite tests for qualifying for the Earned Income Credit are available at the IRS website. Make sure you have all supporting documentation in advance of any inquiry to avoid scrambling. You will need to show it to your preparer as well, who has no interest in paying a penalty because you lied to him or her.

5. TIPS

Waitresses, bartenders, hair stylists – we all know you are tipped. By not declaring your tip income (or just a minimal portion), how substantial do you expect your Social Security check to be when they are averaging your annual income over 35 years? While many folks in these industries are often underpaid, two wrongs don't make a right, and it is tax evasion if you omit this income.

Keep track of your tips; your good records may save you one day, in case the IRS tries to say you received more than you actually did in tips. Contemporaneous records will tip the scale in your favor.

6. UNREPORTED RENTAL PROPERTY

Ah yes, you can thank the neighbor who doesn't appreciate you walking your dog near her property.

Or perhaps the meter reader. If you are not declaring your rental income, there is always someone who will talk to the Tax Authorities.

The omission of rental property on a tax return is a big mistake. Even if there's no gain after expenses such as mortgage interest, real estate taxes, depreciation, etc., it still needs to be reported. In fact, when it comes to depreciation on a rental property, if you were supposed to take it and didn't, the IRS will not give you any consideration for missing it, and will treat the deduction as taken. This is a complex, detailed area, but the takeaway here is that you should declare your rental income and all allowable expenses. Believe it or not, it usually plays out in your favor, and you can now walk your dog anywhere you want (but please clean up after him).

7. FANCY CARS, BOATS

You declare earnings of $25,000, yet you just bought a loaded Model 3 Tesla (think $100,000+) and are trying to claim the $7,500 tax credit. Those loaded plug-in cars can cost a bundle. Hmmm...how were you able to afford that?

Keep in mind that the IRS can do a "lifestyle audit." In this day and age of internet and cross-checking databases, there is no place to hide. You register the car and up pops a record at the DMV. You travel out of the country and there's yet another database. The authorities often communicate with each other.

The authorities now look more closely at travel, and you can potentially lose your passport if you have more serious IRS issues. And in New York State, certain tax problems will cause you to lose your driver's license, and it's a much lower threshold than one would think.

If the IRS is considering a lifestyle audit, they will do a search on you and your activities. In fact, they usually perform searches in preparation for most audits.

But bear in mind it is truly hard to cry poverty to an IRS Auditor when you have expensive toys, are traveling to the lovely beaches of Italy, live in a fancy part of town, etc. As stated earlier, in our internet world, it's hard to hide.

8. MARIJUANA/DRUGS

An allowable business? In some states, yes, but regardless, legal or not, you still must report income from the sale of it. Deductions may be limited; check with your tax advisor (who hopefully is not a customer).

Certain states have published online tax guides to assist with these businesses. For example, California has made a tax guide available for medical cannabis businesses. Check with your state and the IRS for new developments in this area.

"Do we need to report this to the IRS?"

9. ILLEGAL BUSINESS

All worldwide income is reportable, regardless of what you do. But please, don't come to me to prepare your taxes.

10. LARGE CASH DEPOSITS/ WITHDRAWALS

We all learned from Eliot Spitzer, didn't we? (For those who are not familiar with the story, see next page.) The banks are watching; the check cashing establishments are watching; your neighbors are watching (which is why you see steel bars on the doors and windows of certain houses). And your mattress may not be a great idea for safe deposits.

Certain cash transactions can be a flag.

It's not a problem to deposit cash from your business. It becomes a problem when you don't fill out Form 8300 when there is a deposit of $10,000 or more. And don't think you are being original if you try to break up the deposits into small increments such as $3,000, $3,000 and $4,000 at a time. There are whistleblowers everywhere, including the banks.

The Bank Secrecy Act mandates that for deposits, withdrawals, exchange of currency or other payment or transfer by, through or to a financial institution involving a transaction of currency of more than $10,000, a Currency Transaction Report (CTR) must be filed. And if you think you can avoid the report by structuring smaller deposits, you cannot. Just ask Mr. Spitzer....

For those of us who don't remember 2008, Eliot Spitzer was the governor of New York, and a poster boy for ethics on Wall Street and the financial industry. He was often referred to as the "Sheriff of Wall Street." He made the mistake of withdrawing very large sums of cash from his bank account, and tried to avoid flagging these withdrawals, as the bank would have to report them to the IRS. Unfortunately for Mr. Spitzer, these withdrawals were flagged as suspicious transactions despite his efforts to conceal the activity, and the information was turned over the IRS. The resulting investigation included wiretaps, where it was learned that he was using the funds for a prostitution agency. We also learned a number of sordid details of his "preferences" that most of us could have lived without. Thus ended his political career.

11. OMITTING W-2's

Some omissions are innocent enough. For example, when you are relocated by your company to another state, but you remain at the same company, there may be two parts to your Form W-2 issued by your company to reflect the apportionment of income between states. Make sure you give BOTH to your tax preparer. The same goes for W-2c forms (Corrected Form W-2's). Every tax document has a reason for its existence; you may not understand them, and that's when you need a qualified tax professional.

If you are in a profession such as commercial acting, where you may work for over 20 employers in a year, it is up to you to keep track of your expected W-2's, and to chase them down when you don't receive them. You may not have them all when you go to file your taxes, but it's likely the IRS does.

If you didn't keep perfect records, you can make a request to the IRS for a transcript which will list all of your employers for the tax year. Then you can reach out to any employer directly for a complete copy of your Form W-2.

12. CLERGY

Regardless of your denomination, you are supposed to declare tips and income received for baptisms, funerals, etc. I prepared tax returns for a woman who filed separately from her husband, who was a member of the clergy. She knew her husband wasn't declaring all of his income on his tax return, and wanted no part of it. Scary on many levels.

13. LAWSUIT

If it's not pain and suffering, it's taxable. For example,

if you sued for back wages and received them in your settlement, they would be taxable because the wages were originally taxable. Your lawyer should know the tax rules regarding different types of settlements, but there are some lawyers that do not, and you may not be properly advised. Your attorney may also not be aware that it is necessary to issue you a Form 1099-Miscellaneous for certain settlements that are taxable, but if you received the money and it does not fall into an excludable category, then you must declare it on your tax return. Some settlements have a breakdown noting exactly what is taxable and what is not. But if you are not provided with a breakdown, and if you are taking a stance that your settlement is not taxable, you need to have sufficient proof. Gather it in advance of your tax filing.

14. FOREIGN-EARNED INCOME

Yes, under certain circumstances, you may be able to exclude it, but you must first report it on your U.S. tax return in order to be able to exclude it. As a citizen, Green Card holder or U.S. resident, you are responsible for reporting and paying tax on worldwide income, regardless of where you reside, unless specifically excluded by the Tax Code.

But there are also instances of where a non-U.S. person may have a U.S. filing requirement and could be subject to U.S. income tax based on the number of days you are in the United States and your entry visa. Unless you carefully track your days on certain visas, you may find yourself being considered a U.S. resident for tax purposes, and income earned "back home" must now be reported to the U.S.

This is not an area for the uninformed; find yourself a qualified tax professional with experience in international taxation for U.S. people and non-U.S. people.

15. GREYHOUNDS AND LAS VEGAS

All gambling winnings are reportable, whether or not you receive a Form W-2G. Examples of gambling income include lotteries, raffles, horse races and casinos.

Your losses are deductible ONLY as an itemized deduction, and only up to the amount of winnings. What does this mean? Under most circumstances, you cannot net your winnings from your losses; they are reported separately. You must itemize (file Schedule A) in order to report the losses. It also means that, if you do not qualify to itemize (taking the standard deduction would have a better result), the gambling losses are not used and cannot be used in a different year. Also, large gambling winnings can push you into a higher tax bracket, and you may be in for a surprise at tax time if you don't carefully track this income.

You are required to have documentation to prove your losses. The IRS wants you to have receipts, tickets, and a diary or similar record of your gambling activity.

If you win a significant amount, you will owe taxes to the IRS and State. It's a good idea to have the payer withhold taxes for you, or you can pay estimated taxes so you are not penalized for underpayment of taxes when you prepare your actual tax return.

Another important caveat – if you play online, where is the money held? If it's held outside of the U.S., you may very well be considered to have an interest in a foreign bank account, and have an additional important reporting requirement.

Professional gamblers will report their income and expenses differently than the casual gambler. They can report their expenses without itemizing (filing Schedule A), and they can net their winnings against their losses and expenses. If you are a professional gambler, be prepared to show the IRS that your gambling activity is your trade or business, and that you pursue the activity full time, with regularity, to make income for a living. I'm sure you are not surprised to hear that the IRS has a list of tests to apply to professional gamblers to differentiate them from the casual gambler.

16. BARTER

The internet has certainly made it easier for more bartering agreements. Regardless of the transaction, each side must report the fair market value of goods and services. Not all transactions occur with money, but it's always reportable.

17. COLLECTIBLES

Many years ago, I had a client that stumbled upon a masterpiece at the Salvation Army. Talk about lucky! It was appraised as the real deal, and sold at Sotheby's for a very large amount of money.

When we sell paintings, coins, art, and other collectibles, this is reportable to the IRS. There may be a gain or they may be a loss. When there is a gain, the transaction is taxed at a maximum 28% rate (as of this writing). Don't assume it's 20% long term capital gain when it's a collectible.

18. IDENTITY THEFT

Got a tax notice that mentions a business you don't have, or W-2's from places you never worked at? You can thank rampant identity theft for this.

IDENTITY THEFT IS RAMPANT.

The IRS has procedures in place for dealing with identity theft, and as soon as you are aware of it, get a police report, file a report with the Federal Trade Commission, flag the credit bureaus, alert the IRS, complete their paperwork, and don't forget to reach out to your state Taxing Authority as well.

This will only get worse as the thieves are spoofing IRS notices, and almost everyone has received (or has a relative or friend who received) a phone call from a fake phone number claiming to be the IRS. Live or robocall, these calls can be scary. Hang up immediately on these people, and call the IRS directly if you are unsure the call is fake.

If you receive an email from the IRS, it is 100% fake – the IRS does not contact taxpayers via email. If you receive a notice asking you to send a check with the payee as IRS, it's fake. "IRS" can be easily changed to "MRS" with another name added, in order to clear the bank. All federal checks are made out to "U.S. Treasury", not "IRS." If you are not sure if your notice is legitimate, call the IRS, or ask a tax professional to review it for you.

19. ALIMONY

Alimony counts as income to the person that receives it. The payer gets a tax deduction on his or her tax return for the alimony paid, and the recipient picks it up as income on his or her tax return. If you received alimony and omit reporting it on your tax return, it's an easy crosscheck for the IRS. The payer, who certainly wants the deduction, must report your name and social security number in order to get the deduction. The IRS will compare returns to make sure everything is in order.

20. DIVORCE

Some of the strongest whistleblower cases are spearheaded by a former spouse. Also, former employees, neighbors, former business partners, etc. have become whistleblowers. There are all kinds of divorces and disgruntled people out there. And these people are very happy to share all sorts of information they have about you with the IRS, including diversion of reportable business income, unreported accounts, assets in the names of others, etc.

21. TRANSFERRING YOUR ASSETS TO A RELATIVE OR FRIEND

Transferring assets with the intent to hide them is called a fraudulent conveyance. For example, people getting divorced do it all the time. There are a lot of bright forensic accountants out there who are capable of uncovering hidden assets. If something that has been on previous tax returns suddenly disappears, someone will pick up on that. Also, when you request an installment agreement from the IRS to get an extension of time to pay your taxes, depending on the amount owed, you may have to declare your assets. It is illegal to omit income, assets, etc. on IRS paperwork. Remember – you sign under penalties of perjury.

22. OTHER INCOME

Jury duty – yes, that $40 is reportable. So is that prize money, the sign-up bonus from your bank and winning the lottery.

Do you remember when Oprah gave a car away to each audience member?

Back in 2004, Oprah gave away 276 cars in September to members of her audience. People were laughing, crying, jumping and screaming. And some of this same behavior continued for another reason -- when they learned about the tax bill! For a brand new Pontiac G-Six, with a sticker price $28,500, the tax bill could have been $7,000 (actually more, if you were in a higher tax bracket, and took state and local taxes into account). And this was after Pontiac agreed to pay state sales tax and licensing fees. The winners of the cars were then given three choices: keep the car and pay the tax, sell the car and pay the tax, or forfeit the car.

Boo hoo.....a very nice problem to have!

FOREIGN ISSUES -
The IRS Has a Long Arm!

23. GRANDMA'S BANK ACCOUNT

Are you a signatory on an account overseas for a relative? Time to familiarize yourself with foreign account reporting rules.

It's not a problem having a foreign bank account. It's a problem not REPORTING the foreign bank account.

Even if you are listed on the account just to help out a relative and the funds are not really yours, the IRS may receive information from a foreign country regarding your name that matches up with an unreported overseas account. Something as innocent as helping a relative can cause a huge problem, even if it's not a Swiss bank account holding $200 million.

Learn about the requirements, or find a qualified tax professional who will walk you through the guidelines of ownership, signature authority, financial interest, etc. This can be one of the most expensive tax mistakes you can make.

24. NOT REPORTING YOUR FOREIGN FINANCIAL ACCOUNTS

There are many places on the U.S. tax return that inquire about overseas accounts. The lowest threshold asks if you have a foreign financial account; you need to check "Yes" even if there is a dollar in it. Check "No" and you just committed perjury. Depending on how much you have in your aggregate accounts, you may be surprised to learn how much other reporting there may be, even if you already pay tax on the account overseas.

Worried about double taxation? There may be relief in the form of a foreign tax credit, or a deduction for foreign tax paid on your U.S. tax return. But you cannot escape the reporting.

The types of reportable accounts include but are not limited to: a bank account, brokerage account, pension, foreign trust, etc. Again, it's not a problem to have these accounts, but you must report them. You could potentially face huge penalties, civil and criminal charges, etc. And while the IRS does have amnesty programs available, they will not be open forever, and it's a gamble you don't want to take. There are treaties and TIEAs (tax information exchange agreements) for the Treasury Department to tie you to your overseas account. The technology is in place as well as these agreements between the U.S. and numerous countries.

Many of my clients have the mistaken belief that their pension is not reportable, because they are under retirement age and can't have it now. Of course, this is a flawed argument, and an expensive mistake. While tax practitioners can only report the accounts that our clients tell us about (I always say telepathy is not on my resume), you are advised to discuss this area with your tax advisor, and you should mention EVERY account you have. This includes an account with the equivalent of one hundred U.S. dollars, and an account with three cents, etc. Once you get over the reporting threshold, EVERY account must be reported.

A true story, and one of my favorites -- I know a very nice man who disagreed with me about the U.S./overseas data sharing. He told me that overseas, his name was Luigi, and here in the U.S, it's Louie – they'll never put it together, he said.

And I thought I was the blonde.

25. YOUR GREEN CARD

You came, you took, you left. Most people hold the incorrect belief that all you need to do to keep your

Green Card is to enter the U.S. at least once a year. Not quite true.

There are a number of ways to have a problem. You can lose your permanent resident status by intentionally abandoning it. You can also lose it by moving to another country, intending to live there permanently, being absent from the U.S. for an extended period of time, failing to file tax returns while outside the U.S. for any period, filing your U.S. tax return using the status of non-resident alien, etc.

Border officials will consider your travel as indications that your real place of residence has not been the United States.

You went through a lengthy process to obtain the Green Card and should take all legal measures to keep it. It's a privilege. If you want to continue to live and work in the U.S. and eventually become a U.S. citizen, you need to obey the rules.

It is advised by many that in order to avoid a full-blown inspection, you should return to the U.S. within six months. Note that every rule has exceptions. If you were out of the U.S. for an extended period of time and have an acceptable reason, you may successfully argue to keep your permanent resident status. For example, if you were caring for a sick relative, and the temporary absence lasted longer than you expected, that may be an acceptable excuse for your absence. Be prepared to show evidence regarding the unforeseen circumstances, and you may consider applying to USCIS for a reentry permit.

26. GREEN CARD MARRIAGES

Not just for the movies. Are you filing a joint tax return with a spouse you may not even know? You DO know that you are both responsible for what goes on that tax return, and you are both jointly and severally liable, correct?

While Immigration and the IRS are separate areas, there are times when certain reporting can overlap. And like the movie, as much as you can rehearse, there's always something to trip you up. Personally, I prefer to throw the Green Card marriages out of my office; they fight more the legitimately married couples and that's saying a lot. They are too busy telling each other that they are counting the days to be rid of each other.

27. WHEN IS A SPOUSE NOT A SPOUSE

Are you married overseas, yet declaring yourself single in the U.S.? The IRS doesn't currently track marriages; for now, it's an honor system. But in this day and age of technology, somehow, you will get tripped up. You need to report your correct filing status, and depending on a number of considerations, you will establish whether filing separately or jointly makes the best sense for your taxes.

This goes for same-sex marriages as well. If you are married, you will use the correct filing status of Married Filing Jointly or Married Filing Separately.

One exception for all – there are times when you can use the Head of Household status even when you are still legally married, but you cannot live with your spouse (you must be apart for at least the last 6 months of the tax year), and you must pay over half of the cost of keeping up the home for yourself and a qualifying person (a child, certain relatives, etc.). The guidelines are available at the IRS website www.irs.gov.

28. DOUBLE-DIPPING ON CREDITS AND DEDUCTIONS

It's fine to report your foreign taxes paid and get a deduction for it. It's not fine to take the credit and the deduction for the same money. There are times when you may fully use the deduction for foreign earned income, and you can take a credit on the same tax return. But the income needs to be properly apportioned between the deduction and the credit. Definitely not an area for the uninformed.

29. FOREIGN MUTUAL FUNDS

Reportable – yes, taxable – yes, complicated – yes, yes, yes! A foreign mutual fund is one that is held overseas. This does not include a foreign holding in your U.S. brokerage account.

Of all the foreign financial assets, the reporting of foreign mutual funds can be the most complex. The U.S. discourages overseas investment and there is a penalty regime attached to overseas mutual funds. You may be subject to a special tax on top of all the other ones you have to pay. These are called PFIC's (passive foreign investment companies) and can be a nightmare to calculate and report.

30. ACCIDENTAL TOURIST

Did you know that if you are in the U.S. for more than 125 days each year, you may be considered a U.S. resident for tax purposes? Note that certain visas do have exclusions (i.e., student visa, depending on the number of years in the U.S., etc.), but if you are here long enough during the tax year, even if you are here on vacation, you are considered a resident for tax purposes, and you are paying tax on WORLDWIDE income. Watch your day count and track your travel!

You can come to the U.S., even for medical purposes, for example, and if you are here long enough, depending on your visa, you could be considered a U.S. resident for tax purposes.

I had this exact case where, on an annual basis, a woman (who was a citizen of a foreign country) came to the U.S. for medical treatment for over six months at a time. Fortunately for her, she was able to avoid having to file an annual U.S. tax return because of a tax treaty the U.S. had with her country. Unfortunately for her, there was another U.S. reporting requirement (Report of Foreign Bank and Financial Accounts) that she could not escape, due to different sections of the Tax Code and tax treaty not matching up. And because she was unaware of this filing, there were many delinquent years. She was potentially subject to tens of thousands of dollars in penalties, civil charges, etc. unless she would enter an amnesty program. She decided to go home and stated she would get tax help overseas.

One note – if the medical issue happens when you are in the U.S. and for some reason, you cannot physically leave, you are granted some relief. But the issue would have to originate in the U.S. For example, if you came to the U.S. on vacation and got injured while you were here, if you are unable to leave, that would be a special circumstance. But this is a very different case than someone coming to the U.S. with a medical issue, and then not being able to leave.

31. OVERSEAS RENTAL PROPERTY IS REPORTABLE

Remember, all worldwide income is reportable unless the Tax Code specifically states it is not. Even if you are paying taxes on the same income overseas, it is still subject to reporting and taxation in the U.S. as well. There are allowable credits and exclusions in certain cases, but you cannot escape the required reporting.

The difference between overseas rental property versus U.S. rental property is the depreciation – the foreign rental is depreciated over 40 years, as opposed to 27.5 for residential real estate in the U.S. But regardless of any differences, rental property is reportable no matter where it is, and it must be reported in U.S. dollars.

But enough about my itemized deductions...

SWEET CHARITY

32. MONETARY DONATIONS TO CHARITY

It's wonderful to be charitable. But if your donations seem high in comparison to your income, the IRS may wonder how you had enough money to live. Could there be unreported income?

Your claims may be legitimate, but be prepared to show receipts, cancelled checks, credit card statements, and an acknowledgement letter from the charity. Gone are the days where you could write off up to a certain amount without a requirement to show substantiation.

I remember a new client that started to bang his fist on my desk, demanding I give him "the maximum donation he can have." I asked him for his receipts, and he said he had none. And I gave him the maximum donation he could have - NOTHING. No longer a client of my office, but I'm sure he found an unscrupulous preparer to make something up for him. Sadly, there are shady preparers are out there, and some of them disappear at the first sign of trouble when the client is caught.

33. TIME

You cannot deduct the value of your time or services for work you do for a qualified organization. For example, if you are a lawyer and provide five hours of legal services assisting a qualified charity, your hourly fee is not deductible as a charitable donation. However, you can deduct travel expenses (the IRS provides a deductible amount per mile, or you can figure out your actual cost of gas, oil, etc.).

34. IF YOU WANT BLOOD

Donations of blood to the American Red Cross or blood banks are not deductible. Be happy you did a good deed, and enjoy the cookie and orange juice.

35. POLITICAL CONTRIBUTIONS

These are NOT deemed to be donations for tax purposes. Do not confuse the two. While some of our politicians are charity cases, it's still not deductible. If you are not sure about an organization you are considering contributing to, find out if they are a 501(c)3 organization. The IRS has a list available at their website.

36. GO FUND MY AUDIT

The internet brings all kinds of new situations, and every day is a learning experience. GoFundMe are generally personal campaigns that ask strangers for support. Donations to a single person for a GoFundMe campaign are not tax deductible. Remember, donations are deductible only when they are sent directly to a registered 501(c)3 organization. If you made a donation to a registered charity at GoFundMe, you would be sent a receipt from their charity partner, and the campaign would display a certified charity badge.

37. GUESS THE NUMBER OF JELLY BEANS IN THE JAR

Bought some raffle tickets or lottery tickets from a charitable organization trying to raise money? Played some bingo or some other game of chance in the name of charity? Unfortunately, none of these are deductible as donations.

One important note – most organizations mean well, but certain people cannot and should not be providing tax advice. If you are making a charitable contribution mainly for the purpose of a tax deduction, you need to do your research first. There is certain wording that must appear on the acknowledgement letter.

"Of course these are worth $450!"

Most legitimate charities are aware of this, but from time to time, we still see acknowledgement letters that are incomplete, and on audit, the client can lose the deduction.

38. DONATIONS OF GOODS

"My Jimmy Choo's cost me $900, so I get a deduction for $450," the client insisted. No, you don't. No one will pay $450 for your smelly, used shoes.

Go online and search for the Salvation Army Valuation Guide or Goodwill Valuation Guide, to get an idea of the fair market value of your donated items. Yes, you may get a larger donation for high-end designer items as opposed to "regular" items, but it must be within reason.

For donations of goods (non-monetary donations), you must have a signed, dated receipt from the charity. You are also responsible for having a breakdown of each item you contributed in the donation, and, as mentioned previously, the fair market value. In the case of larger donations, I recommend pictures as well. If you are trying to defend a larger donation, having as much substantiation as you can will only strengthen your position. Gone are the days of "eight bags of clothes, $6,000 donation" scribbled on a receipt.

If the value of the donated property is more than $5,000, you must get a qualified appraisal (this is for property only; not money).

There are also special rules when a vehicle is donated. The amount you may take as a deduction for the charitable donation of a vehicle may be affected by what the charity does with it (sell it and uses the proceeds for the charitable organization; use the vehicle for its charitable activities; fixes up the vehicle and then sells it to use the proceeds for the charitable organization etc.). The IRS website has a wealth of useful information in this area.

FORMS YOU RECEIVED OR SHOULD HAVE FILED

39. FORM 1099-K

You cleaned your house, you sold all of your worldly goods on eBay, and had over 200 transactions. And then the mail arrives. What's a Form 1099-K, you ask?

In a sentence, your sales have just been announced to the IRS. Now they think you have an unreported side business. This can happen with garage sales, rental of your apartment or house (think Airbnb), etc. If you accept online or credit card payments for services, if you are compensated via PayPal, Etsy, eBay, etc., you may receive a Form 1099-K.

Form 1099-K is filed by credit card companies and third party processors (PayPal, Amazon, etc.) to report the payment transactions they process. What triggers this form? There are a number of triggers: credit card companies may file one if the sales volume is over $600 per year; third-party processors will file one if you had over $20,000 in sales and more than 200 individual transactions.

This form, in particular, causes issues for many businesses, as sales reported may not match because of sales tax, timing issues, etc. And it also causes issues for those who thought they didn't have to declare their eBay activities, some of which are businesses in disguise.

By now you must realize that your unassuming side business, house cleaning, or garage sale has put you on the map with the IRS, and omitting this reporting from your tax return will surely generate a correspondence audit at minimum.

40. SALE OF STOCK

You got clobbered in the market and had a loss, so you didn't report the sale. And now you have an IRS notice that rivals "War and Peace." Often, the IRS will give you a zero cost basis, so you will receive a notice assessing taxes due along with interest and penalties. They have calculated what they deem to be additional unreported income and the taxes due on this income, plus interest for not timely paying the taxes, and various penalties for your error. It's up to you to properly report the sale of all securities on Schedule D and the underlying forms, thereby showing the proceeds and the original cost basis of that security, to prove that there was a loss. This is surprisingly a very common occurrence. Some people have a relative trading under their name, or they just honestly forget about the sale of a security during the tax year and ignored the tax form. In many cases I have been involved with, the IRS ended up owing the taxpayer a refund once we properly reported the security's cost basis.

It is the taxpayer's responsibility to keep good records. Many financial institutions have mergers over the years, making it more difficult to locate the original purchases, and they do not have to maintain records for over seven years.

41. GIFT FROM THE OLD COUNTRY

Did you receive a gift from Mom, Dad, Brother, Uncle, or Cousin - whomever - that lives back in the old country? If you receive a gift or inheritance from a non-resident alien (someone who is not a citizen, Green Card holder or U.S. resident) of over $100,000 in a calendar year, you have a filing requirement (Form 3520) to report the gift. This person does not have to be related to you. There are special rules too if you receive smaller gifts from related overseas donors.

This is an information return, not an income tax return. But fail to file this when you should have, or file it late, incomplete, or incorrect, and you can have a serious problem on your hands. The IRS can impose a penalty, and it can be as much as 25% of the gift.

There may be some available relief in this area (amnesty programs, special procedures for information returns that don't have a tax attached to them), and it's best to file the information return with a statement of reasonable cause for your failure to timely file it (in other words, beg for forgiveness). It's always better to step forward first before you are caught.

42. PAYROLL, HOUSEHOLD EMPLOYEES

You have an eligible dependent, and you want to claim a deduction for dependent care on your tax return. You have money withheld via a program at work. So, what's the problem here?

That pre-tax deduction becomes taxable when you file your tax return if you don't report the actual dependent care expense. But wait – you have an off-the-books nanny. How can you report expenses for child care, when you don't even have your nanny's Social Security number because everything is off the books and you pay her in cash? And, of course, she doesn't even have a Social Security number because she is an illegal alien.

You can't have it both ways.

Remember the politicians who found this out the hard way? There were a few high profile cases, and they even nicknamed the situation – Nannygate.

Back in January 1993, corporate lawyer Zoe Baird employed two illegal aliens from Peru as nanny and chauffeur for her child. The following month, federal judge nominee Kimba Wood was also caught for employing undocumented immigrants to look after her child. Both of these women were then-President Bill Clinton's choices for U.S. Attorney General. Another candidate for this position was attorney Charles Ruff, but as he did not pay Social Security taxes for years for a woman who cleaned his house, he was ruled out as well. There have been numerous elected officials who have either hired illegal aliens and/or didn't follow the rules for payroll of household help.

"Why should I care?" you may ask. While you may think that you are not high profile, and you may not have any political aspirations, think about this: Should your nanny trip and fall on the job, and she goes to the Department of Labor to report you, then the IRS can find out, and then the State can find out, and you have a really, really big mess on your hands. And a very expensive one as well.

43. NOMINEE INCOME

I swear I was just holding it for my friend!

If you received a tax form (for example, a Form 1099), reporting income that does not belong to you, you should report the income on your tax return, and reverse it out with an explanation, including the other party's name and Social Security number. Someone needs to pick up the income on their tax return, and this helps the IRS understand who the income actually belongs to.

If you and another person share an account, it's the same situation; you may decide that you each will report 50% of the earnings, but for the person who received the document, you will need to report the total amount and then reduce your income by that 50% which represents nominee income.

44. CANCELLATION OF DEBT

You negotiated with your credit card company to reduce your balance owed. Surprise! You just received a Form 1099-C from the credit card company, reporting the amount you thought you were off the hook for to the IRS.

That difference will be deemed to be income, and

must be declared on your tax return. In certain cases, you may be able to exclude that income (for example, if you are insolvent, bankrupt, etc.). But be prepared to prove your insolvency via Form 982, which needs to be included with your tax return. You may receive relief for the full amount or a partial amount depending on your situation.

45. UNEMPLOYMENT

As if things aren't bad enough when you lose your job, you have to pay tax on your unemployment benefits. People still are shocked that this is the case, and often forget to report it. A few years back, there was a portion of unemployment benefits that were not taxable, but that law is no longer valid as of this writing. Unemployment benefits are federally taxable, and depending on your state, it may be taxable on that level as well.

Your State Department of Labor may ask if you want to have taxes withheld. It's a good idea if you can do it, so you are not faced with a big bill at tax time. But if you need every dollar until you are back on your feet, taxes may need to wait.

46. PENSION CASH-OUTS

After the 2008 market crash, I saw more pension

cash-outs in a single year than I would see over a five-year period. So many people raided their 401(k) accounts, their IRA accounts, etc. And many didn't have the foresight to have any withholding and got a whopping tax bill. Others chose 20% federal withholding (when they were in a much higher tax bracket) and they had no state withholding, and were not happy when they saw the amount they owed. As with unemployment, this happened because people lost their jobs and were in tight spots financially. There was no thought to this process beyond desperately raiding the account earmarked for retirement.

They had no emergency fund and lived paycheck to paycheck. Many were surprised they would be taxed at all. On top of taking away money from yourself so you can eat later in life, the cash-outs put many taxpayers in higher tax brackets, as it is considered income in the year cashed out, and there is a 10% penalty for early withdrawal. Perhaps many thought there was some hardship provision, but most didn't qualify, and not all plans have these provisions.

The moral of the story is that an emergency fund is an absolute must. And if the latest iPhone must wait, so be it.

47. FIRST TIME HOMEBUYER'S CREDIT

Bought a house in 2008 and got the credit? You are still paying back the First Time Homebuyer's Credit, as it was really a 15-year loan.

Perhaps unfairly, another credit was rolled out the following year, which affected homes purchased in 2009, 2010 and 2011, which does not have a payback requirement. As they say, timing is everything.

48. EVERYONE'S A CONSULTANT

"I don't want to pay payroll taxes," says the small business owner. "I'll issue everyone a Form 1099-Miscellaneous because they are contractors." Newsflash – that's not how it works. You can slap a label on anyone, but the IRS may disagree.

You are directing them in how they perform their work, providing desk space, mandating the hours they work, providing equipment, etc. You have an employee, not a contractor.

The IRS has a number of tests to be applied in each case, to see if the worker is a contractor or employee. You may have had all of your "consultants" sign a contract and they do because they need the work and money. But it's a facts-and-circumstances case,

and that contract might not be worth the paper it's written on. There is no one test that is the deal maker or deal breaker, so familiarize yourself with all of the tests, so you can defend your decision.

There was a famous FedEx case involving a lawsuit brought by California workers, which really brings this point home. This case concerned the misclassification of workers, as FedEx classified their drivers as independent contractors. The Ninth Circuit said in a 2014 ruling that FedEx controlled the drivers (didn't they have to wear FedEx uniforms, use FedEx hand-held scanners, etc.?) and ruled against FedEx. This was a $228 million mistake. And it didn't stop there. Two years later, there was a $240 million settlement for drivers in 20 states.

Maybe your situation isn't this big. But if you have one independent contractor who goes to the Department of Labor requesting unemployment benefits, and tells them that s/he was really an employee, you have a big, expensive mess on your hands.

There are companies that put everyone on payroll, even contractors, because they want to be totally safe and take no chances. They feel it's cheaper to make everyone an employee.

49. MORE ON PAYROLL TAXES

Your establishment has four people on the payroll, yet there are seventeen workers on the floor. Uh-huh. Not the least bit original. Or legal.

50. SALE OF YOUR HOME

Yes, there's a $250K exclusion ($500K married filing jointly), for the sale of the personal residence. But it's not as easy as that. IRS Code Section §121 has ownership requirements and usage requirements, too. Make sure you qualify for the exclusion. And if you had to move for work or medical reasons causing you to fail the ownership and usage requirements, there is relief available via an allowable partial exclusion. To avoid paying taxes unnecessarily, when you are calculating any gain, remember to include the allowable closing costs (i.e., legal fees, etc.) of the purchase as well as the sale. You can also include expenses incurred for remodels and improvements to the property.

51. NET INVESTMENT TAX FORM 8960

The form you never heard of. Yes, there can be an additional 3.8% tax on your investments on top of all of the other taxes you pay. So regardless of your "regular" tax bracket, you could potentially be paying significantly more in tax thanks to Form 8960.

52. MORTGAGE INTEREST

Your Manhattan apartment or Hamptons estate may provide you with a deduction for mortgage interest, but when your mortgage is over the $1.1 million mark (combination of your home acquisition debt and home equity debt), a limitation kicks in. See IRS Publication 936 for instructions and details. Hope you enjoy algebra.

There are new rules for unmarried taxpayers where they can each claim their respective deductions giving them each a $1.1 million threshold, unlike married taxpayers who together only get $1.1 million before the limitation starts. As if married people aren't penalized enough.......

53. SOCIAL SECURITY BENEFITS

Are social security benefits taxable? Like most aspects of tax, the answer is "It depends." They can be non-taxable, 50% taxable, or taxed up to 85%. You need to familiarize yourself with the rules. It depends on your combined income, which is defined as your adjusted gross income, tax-exempt interest income and half of your Social Security benefits.

54. YOUR PENSION

Just because your State may deem your pension as non-taxable income, it does not mean the IRS will treat your pension in the same manner. As no one likes a tax bill; make sure you have advised the company administering your pension to withhold the proper taxes if necessary. It's always easier to pay a bill over a number of months, as opposed to writing that lump sum check by April 15th.

55. EDUCATOR EXPENSES

Teachers and other eligible educators are eligible for an above-the-line deduction of up to $250 on the tax return for any unreimbursed classroom expenses. Expenses above the $250 limit can be reported as an itemized deduction on Schedule A. It is limited to a particular grade level (Kindergarten through Grade 12), and you must have receipts.

It is a deduction for teachers, instructors, counselors, principals and aides if you work at least 900 hours in a school year. Keep those receipts – you will need them to support the deduction, and expenses over $250 (as of this writing). These expenses can be reported as an itemized deduction on Schedule A. There are a number of qualified expenses you can deduct including books, supplies, computer equipment, etc.

You are NOT eligible for this above-the-line deduction for College-level teaching.

56. MOVING EXPENSES

While you can deduct your moving expenses when you move for work purposes over fifty miles, there is one important question. Did your company reimburse you? If so, you cannot take the deduction - no double-dipping!

You cannot deduct expenses for buying or selling a home, expenses to enter into or break a lease, loss on the sale of your home, pre-move house hunting expenses, etc.

You can deduct moving expenses for yourself and members of your household. This includes the cost of packing, crating and transporting your personal effects, shipping your car and pets, one month of storage, the cost of transportation and lodging for you and your family, etc. And of course, the IRS says that your expenses must be reasonable.

Your relocation must relate to starting a new job or a transfer to a new location for your present employer.

Moving outside of the U.S.? You must meet the same tests as a U.S. move, but if you claim the foreign earned income or foreign housing exclusion, you cannot deduct the part of the moving expenses that relates to the excluded income. IRS Publication 54 has all the details.

57. INHERITANCES OF IRAs

Not reporting distributions on an inherited IRA is a mistake and an IRS notice will be generated. Inherited IRAs come with a number of rules, regulations and reporting requirements. And mistakes are expensive. There is different tax treatment if you are the spouse of the decedent, as opposed to another relative.

Life insurance proceeds are not taxable, generally speaking, and are not to be confused with inherited IRAs.

Inheriting an annuity? Definitely contact an expert. There are various types of annuities, some taxable, some partially taxable, etc. And if it's not confusing enough, some states have different tax treatment that deviate from the IRS.

58. 529 WITHDRAWALS

Unless the money you withdraw from a 529 education account is used specifically for education, it will be taxable. If you receive a Form 1099-Q, you must report what funds were used for education. Omit it and there may be an inquiry. There are also rules regarding the withdrawals and taking other education credits, so read up and arm yourself with knowledge. Make sure you understand the rules. No one wants to pay back money to the IRS, especially with interest and penalties.

59. SCHOLARSHIPS

Not all scholarships are tax-free. Your scholarship or fellowship grant is tax-free and 100% excludable from gross income only if you are a candidate for a degree at an eligible educational institution. The grant cannot exceed your qualified education expenses, and it cannot be designated for room and board.

If your scholarship represents payment for services such as teaching or research, it generally will be taxable. There are exceptions, so educate yourself (sorry...had to put that in) and make sure you understand the IRS definitions of qualified education expenses, candidate for degree, eligible education institution, etc.

60. FORM K-1

If you are a partner in a partnership or a shareholder in an S Corp, you cannot file your tax return without your K-1. Historically, companies can be slow to provide these forms, because they need to do their own tax returns to generate the form. Many of these companies will file a request for an extension of time to prepare their returns, and therefore you will need to file an extension and wait until they actually deliver the K-1 to you.

But wait -- you want your refund now, so you are thinking about filing before April 15th and then amending the tax return later when the form arrives. That's a problem. As much as you want your refund, you cannot file without this form if you know there is something reportable. When you file a tax return, you are signing under the penalty of perjury that the return is complete. And since you have knowledge that it is not complete, do not file.

NO, THAT'S NOT DEDUCTIBLE

61. COSMETIC SURGERY

My teeth, my nose, my breasts! Unless you can truly prove that your medical expense was medically necessary, those capped teeth or DDDs are not DDDdeductible.

You may be thinking of a case of an exotic dancer, Cynthia Hess, who was able to convince the Tax Court that she should be allowed to deduct her implants. However, she did not receive a medical deduction for them. Ms. Hess successfully convinced the court that her implants were stage props and business assets, and that they improved her ability to earn income, with no personal benefit derived from them. She received a business deduction.

62.   CHILD SUPPORT

Child support is not deductible. It is not the same as alimony (spousal support). It is not deductible by the payer, nor taxable to the payee. It's important to properly characterize in your marital settlement agreement exactly what is child support and what is spousal support.

63. COMMUTING TO WORK

This is basic Tax Law 101. We all need to get to work, and there is no deduction for it. If your work requires travel between offices, meetings, special locations – that would be deductible, generally speaking. But traveling to and from your everyday job – no. If it was, I'd make sure there would be a limo out front every day.

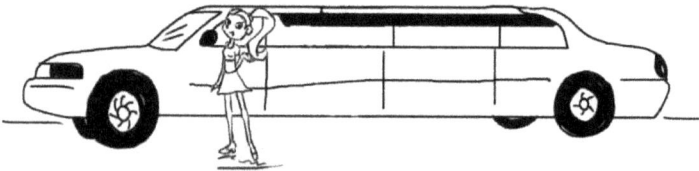

64. UNIFORMS

"I'm a bartender so my black top and pants are my uniform." Uh-huh. Because your friend told you so. This just gets better.

A uniform is defined as clothing that is not suitable for everyday wear. And sewing a patch of your company's logo to your blazer doesn't cut it either. Allowable uniforms are based on your occupation, and the assumption is that if you are a nurse, firefighter or police officer, you would not wear your uniform when off duty.

On the topic of clothing required by your employer, and necessary for your job – one word to the wise – if you are going into Tax Court to defend your position about work clothing being ordinary and necessary for your job, DO NOT wear it to court. While the IRS may allow a deduction for protective clothing as a construction worker, showing up to court in your steel-toed boots may throw your case. Imagine if the judge asks you if you are wearing them!

65. CLOTHING DEDUCTION FOR ACTORS AND ENTERTAINERS

"I would NEVER wear a white blouse – it was just for my go-see." This was an actual comment made in my office by an actress client, in her quasi-Shakespearian voice. She was insisting on a deduction for her white, button down blouse.

If you can wear it on the street, this deduction you will eat. Apologies to the Estate of Johnny Cochran.

66. MY NAILS

"I have to look nice at work." "Blowouts are a must – my hair has to look terrific." "I have to dry clean my regular business clothing."

These items are called maintenance, and even for people in entertainment (think hair extensions, facials, etc.), they are NOT an allowable deduction. They are all considered a personal expense by the IRS.

Years ago, haircuts were an allowable deduction in certain professions, but today, it's not even a deduction for a police officer.

However, if you do have an actual uniform such as a police uniform, etc., you are allowed a deduction for the cleaning of these items. Keep these receipts separate from your personal items, or do a really good job at tracking personal vs. work-related expenses, so you will have no issues with your deduction.

67. MY WORK CLOTHES

"I'm an executive. I need to wear expensive suits." Or, "My employer insists that I buy the clothing of the company and wear these items when I'm working."

Unfortunately, even though certain items may be mandated by the employer, they are not deductible on the tax return. In April 2016, the Tax Court handed down an unfavorable decision (now known as the Ralph Lauren case).

A salesman at Ralph Lauren was required to wear head-to-toe Ralph Lauren clothing at all times, while representing the company. This was even a condition of his employment. The salesman viewed these required purchases as a work-related tax deduction. Unfortunately, the IRS denied the deduction, and the case went all the way to Tax Court. And the taxpayer lost the case. The clothing failed one of the three established criteria that an employee must satisfy before the deduction would be allowable – unsuitable for wear outside of work.

In my office, we see this often with young ladies recently out of school in sales positions at the local mall, where they are forced to buy and wear clothing of their employer. While they do get an employee discount, it's always an unwelcome surprise when they learn they do not get a tax deduction. Unfair, but it's the law.

This is a tax deduction, right?

68. TICKETS, PENALTIES

Do you really think you get a tax deduction for breaking the law, paying your taxes late, or making a mistake? My clients come to me and drop their parking tickets on my desk, and I promptly hand them back. You do not receive a tax deduction, even for a business vehicle, for traffic tickets.

Many people who report their prior year's state taxes paid as a deduction on their Schedule A often pick up the wrong number – the allowable deduction is for taxes only; penalties and interest cannot be included.

69. GYM MEMBERSHIP/POOL/SPECIAL FOOD

None of these are allowable deductions on your tax return UNLESS you have an actual prescription. Not a recommendation from the doctor, but a written prescription.

Sounds easy, but the IRS will want to know that any of these expenses are for the diagnosis, cure, mitigation, treatment or prevention of disease, and the costs of treatments affecting any part of function of the body.

You also must prove that the primary use is medical, and even with a prescription, you still may find yourself having to prove to the IRS that your claim is legitimate.

You may need to get appraisals of your property before and after the installation of a pool, in order to figure your deduction. But one silver lining is that you can write off operational and upkeep expenses as long as the main medical reason for installing the pool remains.

70. MISCELLANEOUS

Never use this word on a tax return.

I see this all the time, especially when self-employed people are listing their expenses. Break out the actual categories of items you are trying to lump together. Do you think the IRS really likes to guess?

And do you truly believe that YOU will remember what you meant by "miscellaneous" in a few years?

While the IRS is less concerned with the category name, they do want to see that you can substantiate anything you put on the tax return. And "miscellaneous" would make someone want to dig deeper. Don't give them a shovel.

71. NON-CUSTODIAL PARENT

You and your former spouse may have an agreement regarding who can claim the dependency exemption for their child on their respective tax returns. It may change for certain years. The agreement may be a divorce decree, or something more informal.

There are several financial benefits to claiming a child as a dependent on the tax return – there is a dependency exemption, the child tax credit, the dependent care credit, head of household filing status, Earned Income Credit, etc. This can add up to thousands of dollars.

Some former spouses ignore the divorce decree or other agreements (I know, big surprise). The IRS is not there to defend a divorce decree, and the former spouses must agree who takes the child.

If the non-custodial parent will be claiming the child, the custodial parent must provide Form 8332 or a similar statement to release the exemption to the non-custodial parent.

What happens when the parents don't agree? If you both claim the same child, one tax return will be rejected. The IRS will subject both of you to tiebreaker rules. You may have a decree, which states in writing, who may claim the child (i.e., parents alternate odd/even years), but it doesn't guarantee the tax treatment with the IRS; they may apply other rules.

The takeaway here is that it's always best to work it out between spouses, because you may be surprised at the outcome, regardless of a written decree. Alternately, you can try to have the courts enforce it, but that can be expensive.

72. PERSONAL CELL PHONE, HOME INTERNET

If you make a few business calls on your cell phone, that does not make it a deductible business phone. You probably have an unlimited plan, so the business usage didn't even cost you anything. If you want to deduct a business cell phone, you should have a separate line for personal calls, and should you be audited, you will have two separate bills to show the auditor. This holds a lot more water than trying to deduct your personal line.

Everyone has internet service these days. And of course there is personal usage to it. And, like your cell phone, there is no additional cost to you to use the internet you already have in place for a little business work. Unless you can show that there is an additional cost (for example, you upgrade to a higher speed, which you would not normally need to have if not for your business), there's little chance this deduction will survive an audit. Sure, there are some auditors that may give you part of the deduction, but it's not the norm.

And if you have bundled phone, internet, cable – forget it. IRS regulations specifically call out bundled services, and they are not deductible. If you have a business with a separate location (think storefront), that's fine, but trying to write this off for your home won't make it past most auditors.

73. HOME OFFICE

When is your bedroom not a bedroom? NEVER!

You may work at home, but that doesn't guarantee the Home Office deduction. In order to claim the Home Office deduction, you must qualify under the exclusive test: You must use a specific area of your home only for your trade or business.

This means that you cannot claim that your dining room table is your office, and then you clean off the papers and have dinner. Nor can you claim your bedroom, because you do work on your laptop, watching TV, etc.

The home office must pass the following tests:

- You must regularly use part of your home exclusively for conducting business.

- You must show that you use your home as your principal place of business. If you conduct business at a location outside of your home, but also use your home substantially and regularly to conduct business, you may qualify for a home office deduction.

If you have a second bedroom used solely for business, then it passes the exclusive test. But it can't be a part-time guest bedroom, laundry room, etc., because it fails the exclusive test.

The office does not have to be walled either. There are other configurations that will pass the test. But doing work in your bedroom doesn't make it a home office.

There are different rules if you are employee, as opposed to someone who is self-employed. More about employees a bit later.

For those who think back to the old days and are afraid the home office deduction is a red flag, those days are over. Many people are self-employed and work at home. Others have employers in different states, and in the employment contract, some employers even pay for the employee's home office expenses.

The IRS has a simplified home office deduction, which requires a great deal less recordkeeping, and is even less of a red flag. All you need to do is to work out the square footage of the office, as opposed to the having to work out the size of your entire property and other expenses.

74. MY LAPTOP, MY IPAD

"I need it for work," says the employee. Is it company policy (written) that you must buy these items out-of-pocket yet not be reimbursed by the company? The tax code states that you can deduct items that are ordinary, reasonable and necessary. But the IRS will also inquire why your employer will not reimburse you if it's so necessary. I have fought this point many times.

One of my cases was an audit of a taxpayer who was a systems engineer. He was directed by his company to have a computer at home, which they would not supply and he would have to obtain and maintain on his own. Unfortunately, they didn't have a written reimbursement policy, and his supporting paperwork was limited. When the employee was audited by the IRS, the company wrote a letter on his behalf, but it was weak and the IRS still didn't allow the deduction. And the employee made a mistake which was a major strike against him - he purchased the computer and had it shipped to someone else! The IRS saw a receipt with a different name and mailing address which was a big red flag to them. The taxpayer thought it would be safer since he wasn't home during the day. Something that sounds like a no-brainer turned out to be a real problem for this taxpayer.

I had another audit where the IRS examiner refused to allow the taxpayer a deduction for her phone data plan. This case was a few years back, before the more common unlimited plans we now have. The taxpayer had irrefutable proof that it was a work requirement, and the non-profit she worked for had a policy that it would not be reimbursed. The taxpayer had to be on call all hours of the day and night. The IRS examiner told me that he himself was required to have a data plan on his phone, yet the IRS won't reimburse him, so why should my client get the deduction? After we argued the point back and forth, I asked him if he really thought my client was playing Angry Birds all day, or answering the calls day and night in the emergency situations she handled. Fortunately, he had a sense of humor, and at the end of the day, he did see the light and we got the deduction. But most people are not prepared to defend these deductions, and need to think about how much they may need to spend to win the point on audit. There are no guarantees on an audit.

75. HOME OFFICE AS AN EMPLOYEE

You take work home consistently and you want a deduction. Sounds logical, right? Nope – not if your employer makes desk space available to you.

There is a rule called the "convenience of the employer" test. If you are going home for your convenience instead of staying at work, then the home office is not deductible. Why? According to the IRS, your use of a home office is "merely appropriate and helpful."

Let's talk a bit more about the convenience test. If a teacher is grading tests at home in a bona fide space that would qualify for the home office test, s/he would still not receive the deduction, because s/he could have stayed at the school and done the work there. Working at home was for the employee's convenience in this case. Same scenario for an attorney who is an employee, reading briefs in his den at home.

If your employer doesn't offer office space and you are required to work at home, then you have a much stronger case (but your office space must still pass the mutually exclusive use test). For example, if your employer is 500 miles away, and has a written policy where you are directed to work at home, that would generally qualify for the home office deduction as an employee.

76. SOLAR POWER CREDITS, ENERGY AND HOME CREDITS

Never forget this important fact: A salesperson will tell you ANYTHING to get you to make a purchase.

Best practices suggestion: We don't take tax advice from salesmen, barbers, janitors, or doormen unless they are also credentialed tax preparers.

If you made a purchase that has a potential tax credit, you need to make sure your tax credit is still in force. For example, with plug-in vehicles, depending on the manufacturer, there is a phase out when a certain number of cars have been sold. Many credits expire, others get extended.

It's best to make a purchase based on your reasons for wanting the actual item, and if you get a deduction or credit for it, that's icing on the cake. Don't depend on something you may not receive.

77. DEDUCTION FOR HEALTH INSURANCE AS AN EMPLOYEE

If your health insurance premium was deducted pre-tax at work (check your paystub), you cannot double-dip and take another tax deduction. If the health insurance premium was out-of-pocket or purchased on the Exchange, it's potentially a deduction for you. As of this writing, there may be major changes on this front. Stay tuned for IRS updates on this matter.

78. BUSINESS MEALS AND ENTERTAINMENT

Here's what is not acceptable to the IRS – you take your friend out, then he takes you out, and then you take him out and then you take him out (rinse and repeat, over and over). This will not fly with the IRS.

An allowable deduction for meals and entertainment must have a valid business purpose. You need receipts and must have documentation that states the name of the person you met with, the company (if applicable) and a brief description of the business purpose. You can use a meal log, tape your receipts to paper with an explanation or keep it digitally. As long as you can produce the substantiation at audit, you can defend the deduction.

79. BUSINESS GIFTS OVER $25

This one's always a shocker to taxpayers. The IRS limits the deduction for a business gift to $25 per person, per year. Want to buy me a Louis Vuitton bag and you are a business associate of mine? Thank you; and remember to take your $25 deduction.

80. INSURANCE

Life insurance (unless part of alimony) is not deductible; it is a personal expense. Same for disability insurance premiums. Long-term care insurance is deductible. Do not confuse the different types of insurance.

If you are a business owner, insurance that you provide for your employees may be deductible as it's a business expense and it could include life insurance, etc.

81. CREDIT CARD INTEREST

Many years ago, you were able to deduct your personal credit card interest. Those days are gone. Now, unless you have a business and the interest is specifically for business expenses, there is no deduction. Another reason not to commingle personal and business expenses on the same credit card.

82. SALY

There is no SAME AS LAST YEAR. Do not tell your preparer SALY, or look at the ceiling for numbers. Do yourself a favor and calculate your actual expenses. There are always changes each year, and if you are not keeping track, you don't get a deduction. It is your responsibility to track your income and expenses.

MISTAKES ON YOUR TAX RETURN – INTENTIONAL OR NOT

83. YOUR NAME – IT DOESN'T MATCH YOUR SOCIAL SECURITY CARD

You got married or you got divorced, or want to use a version of your legal name. The mismatch will cause an inquiry or a rejection of your tax return. When you prepare your return, you must use the legal name as it appears on your Social Security card. If you have a life change, advise the Social Security Administration to update your record.

84. YOUR SOCIAL SECURITY NUMBER

45 becomes 54 – we all make typos. This one means that the IRS can't match you up to their records. This can also cause an electronic filing rejection. Employers make mistakes too. Take the time to look at a recent paystub, and make sure everything is in order before tax time.

85. DEPENDENTS

Your spouse, as childish as he or she may be, is NEVER your dependent. You may file jointly with your spouse, even if it's a non-working spouse. But watch the terminology.

86. HEAD OF HOUSEHOLD STATUS

"I pay my rent and utility bills – aren't I Head of Household?"

Please get your filing status correct. If you are single, with no dependents, you file as Single. You are not Head of Household unless you are considered unmarried for tax purposes, which the IRS defines as filing a separate return, paying more than half the cost of keeping up a home for the year, living apart from a spouse during the entire last six months of the tax year, and providing a main home for more than half the year of dependent child, stepchild, or foster child. If you are unmarried, you may be able to use a grandchild, niece or nephew as a qualifying child for Head of Household. If you are married, you cannot include grandchildren, brothers, sisters or their descendants.

Also, you may qualify as Head of Household if you provide support for your parents. Note that they do not have to live with you. I just heard a sigh of relief somewhere.....

The IRS website (www.irs.gov) has a wealth of information on filing status and almost every conceivable tax situation. Better to use it as a definitive reference rather than asking your friend who knows less than you.

87. FUDGING YOUR BUSINESS NUMBERS TO QUALIFY FOR A MORTGAGE

Many taxpayers are under the mistaken notion that you can omit some or all of your business expenses now, because you want to show higher net income to qualify for a mortgage, and later amend your return afterwards to include the expenses and reduce your income. You can't have it both ways. It's called fraud. You must report all of your business income and expenses. And yes, it's the law.

88. EDUCATION

After years of taxpayers reporting fraudulent classes they really didn't take, the IRS now requires proof for the education credits and deduction. And because of new penalties the IRS can assess, your tax preparer will ask you too. On inquiry by the IRS, you will be asked to present Form 1098-T (tuition statement generated by the school) AND proof of your payments. Locate your credit card payments, cancelled checks, proof of your student loan applied to your bill, or ask the Bursar to provide you with a statement of your payments. Rampant cases of fraud and identity theft have caused the IRS to step up and get tougher in certain areas, and this is one of them.

89. REAL ESTATE PROFESSIONAL

Everyone with more than one rental property decides he or she is a real estate professional. Why? For the tax deduction, of course.

Based on adjusted gross income and how much you participate in the rental real estate activity, the rental deduction for a non-professional can be limited or suspended until the rental unit is sold. So everyone thinks it's better to be a real estate professional. The IRS even created a training manual on how to audit real estate professionals, so you had better be sure you truly qualify for this designation. They will look at how many hours you spend on managing the properties (material participation), other work you do (do you depend on another job for your income?), and apply a number of tests to determine your situation.

"Do you think we can borrow the neighbors' children"?

90.   WHEN KIDS AREN'T YOUR KIDS

Gone are the days when you could easily get away with putting down your neighbor's kids or the children of some relative as a dependent on your tax return. This also ties into EIC fraud.

For anyone you claim on your tax return, s/he must pass the test as a dependent based on the Tax Code. The IRS provides a flow chart as well as all of the qualifying tests at their website. Make sure your dependent can legally be deducted as a "qualifying child" or "qualifying relative." Not every friend you support, who sleeps on your couch, qualifies as a dependent.

"Can we deduct the dog"?

91. PETS

Unfortunately, as much as we spend on our pets, who are truly family members, their medical expenses are not deductible. Congressman McCotter introduced a bill in 2009 to enact this into law, but to no avail. Talk to pet owners and you will hear about the thousands of dollars people spend out-of-pocket for their pet's medical care. Maybe one day...

92. DEDUCTING AN IRA WITHOUT MAKING THE ACTUAL CONTRIBUTION

Certain taxpayers may receive a deduction on their tax returns for making Traditional IRA contributions and/or SEP IRA contributions. That's all well and good, but you must actually make the contribution before the deadline. How does the IRS know? The following year, a Form 5498 will be issued by the IRA custodian (bank or other financial institution), which reports your total annual contributions to an IRA account. Be mindful of the deadlines – you have until April 15th of the following year to make an IRA contribution. If you file a timely extension request and you are a sole proprietor, you have until October 15th of the following year to make a SEP IRA contribution. There are no extensions for Traditional or Roth IRA contributions, and after October 15th, it's all over for SEP IRA's for the prior year.

93. SIDE BUSINESSES WITH LOSSES EVERY YEAR

I had a client (former client, now) who bragged that she reported a side business with a loss for 20 years.

The expectation of running a business is that you operate it with a profit motive. Your hobby does not get the same tax treatment as a business – you cannot write off expenses beyond income, nor are they reported in the same manner. If you haven't made ANY profit in decades, that's a good indication that you have no profit motive, no business acumen, and it's time to shut down. Or admit that it's a hobby, not a business.

Businesses can have losses, and while there are guidelines as to how long a business can report losses, there is no actual law. The circumstances of your losses will be considered; you may have a lot to defend in front of an IRS examiner. But twenty years – that just means that the client hasn't been caught...yet. While the IRS can't catch everybody, sometimes it's just a matter of time.

94. GOOD SPOUSE, BAD SPOUSE – IS YOUR SPOUSE A LOUSE?

Is your spouse hiring illegal workers, or doing some crazy unethical things in his business? Don't file jointly with your spouse! You could potentially be responsible for some (or even all) of the liability if you choose the filing status of married filing jointly. There are certain ways to separate your liability from your spouse, but there are forms to file, hoops to jump through and, of course, contact with the IRS.

There are three types of relief from joint and several liabilities for spouses who filed joint returns:

- Innocent Spouse Relief provides relief from additional tax you would owe if your spouse or former spouse failed to report income, reported income improperly or claimed improper deductions or credits.

- Separation of Liability Relief provides for the allocation of additional tax owed between you and your former spouse or your current spouse from whom you are separated when an item was not reported properly on a joint return. The tax allocated to you is the amount for which you are responsible.

- Equitable Relief may apply when you do not qualify for innocent spouse relief or separation of liability relief for something not reported properly on a joint return and generally attributable to your spouse. You may also qualify for equitable relief if the amount of tax reported is correct on your joint return but the tax was not paid with the return.

Rest assured that your tax and financial activities will likely come into question as well.

You may have also heard of Injured Spouse Relief, but this is different than Innocent Spouse Relief as described above. Injured Spouse Relief is requested when you file a joint return and all or part of your refund is applied against your spouse's past due federal or state tax, child or spousal support, student loan debt, etc.

95. THEFT AND CASUALTY

I lost my Faberge egg and Ming vase.

This is an area frequently questioned by the IRS. You need to show proof of the theft or casualty, the fair market value of the item prior to the theft or casualty, what you did in terms of insurance (wait...you say you didn't put the claim through insurance, but you want to try to deduct it on your tax return?), if you received reimbursement, etc. You do not get replacement value, and there is a bit of a haircut as well – you must itemize (file Schedule A), deduct $100 from each casualty or theft event, and subtract 10% of your adjusted gross income from that total to calculate your allowable casualty and theft losses for the year.

The IRS has published some helpful theft and casualty workbooks for personal use and business use property, and in this day and age of frequent hurricanes and other disasters, it's a good idea to become familiar with them. They are available at no charge at their website: www.irs.gov.

96. PERSONAL EVENTS MASQUARADING AS BUSINESS EVENTS

"My daughter's wedding is a business expense because I invited my client list." Uh – no, it's not.

Same goes for trips that are predominantly personal vacations. These are limitations in reporting the business portion. More on this shortly.

97. PERSONAL DEDUCTION FOR SECURITY

"I want to deduct my dogs – I live in a bad neighborhood." It's actually a great idea, but sadly, not deductible and is a personal expense.

However, this can be an allowable deduction for a business. If your guard dog watches over inventory, etc., it is a deduction.

Back to the personal front, while a deduction for personal security is not available, there are deductions available for dogs used as guide dogs and service animals. There are charitable deductions available for those who foster and rescue animals for an IRS-approved charity. And if you deduct state/local sales tax on your Schedule A, you may be able to deduct the sales tax paid on pet food.

98. EDUCATION AND TRAVEL

"I'm an art teacher – my honeymoon in Italy to visit museums for research is a deductible business expense." The answer (after clutching my sides from much laughing): Travel as a form of education is not deductible.

This was an actual case. There was a taxpayer who signed a tax return with this exact deduction on it (not prepared by my office, of course), and I was representing her in the audit. Another colleague asked me to take the case, because he knew it would be quite a fight. Her return was flagged for questioning by the IRS because of this very deduction insisted upon by a poorly chosen tax preparer, who was a real estate attorney moonlighting as a tax preparer. Not only was this taxpayer being audited, but many of her friends who were clients of this attorney/tax preparer had been audited as well. We did quite well for the client, but her tax problem never should have happened.

While on topic, it's a good time to discuss preparer fraud again. When the IRS sees frequent mistakes from the same preparer, they will audit the taxpayers and pay a visit to the preparer as well.

In cases of serious preparer fraud, the Feds come into the preparer's office and haul away his or her files and computers to have a much closer look. We have seen this for a number of clients who come to us because they are being audited, and it's especially sad when it's a taxpayer who is not knowledgeable in tax law. They were relying on the preparer for their expertise and ethics, and they were certainly let down. The refunds they received were quickly spent, and now they have to pay it back, often for multiple years, with penalties and interest. When we know the problem was caused by the actions of the preparer, we do try to get penalties abated. But remember – an audit can be a long, expensive process, and taxpayers are advised to not only be careful with who they choose to prepare their return, but to take the time and read their tax return (which is one of the most important financial documents you have). If there's anything that stands out (like a preparer trying to deduct coats, clothing, honeymoons, etc.), it's best to deal with it before it becomes a bigger problem.

99. CRAZY SCHEDULE A's or "I TOLD HIM NOT TO PUT THAT DOWN"

If you know your preparer has padded your tax return with blatantly fake deductions, do not sign! Take your original documents and run.

I have seen tax returns chosen for examination with the craziest deductions. (I told one client, "I didn't know handbags were deductible! I'm off to Gucci!") When I ask the taxpayer why he or she would sign this return, I hear, "I told him not to put that down."

When you sign the tax return, you are agreeing under the penalty of perjury that everything on the tax return is correct and valid. Even if the tax authorities don't catch you directly, as noted previously, they may one day catch up with the rogue preparer, and audit ALL of his prepared returns.

I represented a police detective who was being audited. He told me that when he went to the former preparer for a copy of his return, the Feds were there hauling out boxes. Now, if that's not an indication.......

100. BUSINESS TRAVEL

Here's one that is based on a true case.

Client: I'm an attorney and want to branch out into real estate. I am taking a real estate course at a resort in Jamaica. The flyer says it's deductible.

Me: Giggles.

Make sure you get your tax advice from a reputable source......please. I know this has been mentioned before, but I cannot stress this enough. The auditor who reviewed the taxpayer's self-prepared return that included this deduction didn't find it as funny as I did, and threw out the deduction.

There are people who will tell your cruises and vacation travel will be tax deductible. There are instances where it can be, but again, get your tax advice from a credentialed preparer, not someone who has

All I said was did you remember to mail your 1040-ES yesterday?

a vested interest in selling you a trip, unless they are willing to pay for your audit. Just tell me where to send my invoice.

If you are claiming a business trip, be prepared to show an itinerary of who you met with, the business purpose of your trip, how long you spent conducting business activities, etc. Best practices – have an itinerary for yourself that shows your flights and business activities for each day, proof of travel such as your plane tickets or train tickets, attach flyers for the seminars or trade show you attended, business cards of associates you met with, etc.

Trips that are a combination of business and personal activities must be apportioned, and there are special rules for travel outside of the U.S.

101. WHEN YOU PAY YOU ESTIMATED TAXES OR BALANCE PAYMENTS UNDER YOUR SPOUSE'S NUMBER

Oddly enough, the IRS has a bifurcated system. If one spouse who is listed as the second spouse on the tax return makes payments and uses his or her Social Security number, it doesn't match up with the account under the lead Social Security number, and notices are generated accusing the taxpayers of unpaid taxes. While an easy fix (if you call the IRS and explain the situation, they will move the money over so it is properly applied), you are still stuck calling the IRS, waiting on hold, explaining the problem, etc.

CONCLUSION

The biggest takeaway is that it's ultimately easier to do the right thing and not have constant worry, always looking over your shoulder. And if something doesn't feel right, question it. Especially if you use a paid tax professional.

Most people want to do the right thing, but the tax law is confusing, difficult to read and ever-changing. Many of your better tax preparers take over one hundred hours of continuing education each year just to keep up with the law (which can even change in the middle of tax season), and these are people who have made taxes their life's work.

There's always a politician saying that he or she will simplify tax code, but there are too many lobby groups out there that will make sure that doesn't happen. For now, this remains to be seen.

It's difficult for the lay person to sit down once a year and do their taxes. There are so many forms and publications to read, and new laws to familiarize yourself with. And there is software that asks you hundreds of questions until your head is spinning. I fix more self-prepared tax returns than you could imagine. And when I talk to these taxpayers and ask what happened, they say that they didn't understand the question. So if you don't understand the question, how will you get the right answer? As my first brilliant mentor (my dad) often said to me: Garbage in, garbage out.

Yes, we all make mistakes. And anyone, even the most learned of tax professionals can (you try doing this for four months straight without a day off, working 20-hour days, hundreds of emails a day demanding your attention, and phones ringing off the hook, clients crying because they won't take responsibility for the financial mistakes they made during the tax year, etc.). One wouldn't think so, but this is a physically and mentally demanding job, not for the faint-of-heart.

There's nothing wrong with educating yourself, so you can work in tandem with your tax professional. Knowledge is power and can only work in your favor. It can only make you smarter, perhaps even making you more comfortable with tax law, and you will save time, money and grief.

Taxes are something to think about year-round, not just in April. The smart moves you make today (properly adjusting your withholding at work, increasing your retirement saving to defer money to a time when you are in a lower tax bracket, etc.) will truly make a difference tomorrow.

I hope you enjoyed this book, and it gave you some food for thought. And a few laughs along the way. If there are any topics you would like to suggest for a forthcoming book, please email us at team@reallifetaxadvice.com.

RESOURCES

The IRS website has publications, forms, and instructions available. Please visit www.irs.gov. Also, your State will have similar information available. There can be variations between federal (IRS) and State reporting, so it's prudent to familiarize yourself with your filing requirements for both.

❧

Do you need a tax professional? Enrolled Agents are America's Tax Experts. Visit taxexpert.naea.org.

❧

Enrolled Agent Credential

The Enrolled Agent credential is an elite credential issued by the Internal Revenue Service (Department of Treasury) to tax professionals who demonstrate special competence in federal tax planning, individual and business tax return preparation and representation matters. Enrolled Agents have unlimited representation rights, allowing them to represent any client before the IRS on any tax matter.

ABOUT THE AUTHOR

Abby Eisenkraft is the CEO of Choice Tax Solutions Inc. She is a federally licensed Enrolled Agent (EA), an Accredited Tax Advisor (ATA), Accredited Tax Preparer (ATP) and a Chartered Retirement Planning Counselor (CRPC).

Abby started her career in tax as a preparer, and quickly gained a reputation for successfully dealing with difficult tax problems, including those previously unsolvable by other tax professionals. She currently specializes in tax controversy cases such as federal and state tax audits, non-filer cases, residency audits, international matters, etc.

Abby is passionate about defending taxpayer's rights before the IRS and State Taxing Authorities. She is a speaker on various tax and financial topics to both the public as well as tax and accounting organizations, a consultant (specializing in the self-employed), and is often quoted in the press and on television as a tax and financial expert.

Free Gift!

Visit RealLifeTaxAdvice.com
for your free bonus!

ULTIMATE
TAX
CHECKLIST

10 THINGS YOU MUST DO
BEFORE
SUBMITTING YOUR TAX RETURN

*9 7 8 0 6 9 2 8 2 4 5 7 3 *